D1390181

EXPLORES ...

THE VIKINGS

Aberdeenshire Library and Information Service
www.aberdeenshire.gov.uk/libraries
Renewals Hotline 01224 661511

MALAM, John

Exploring the Vikings

REMAINS TO BE SEEN
EXPLORING THE VIKINGS

JOHN MALAM

EVANS BROTHERS LIMITED

First published in paperback in 2003
Evans Brothers Limited
2A Portman Mansions
Chiltern Street
London W1U 6NR
Reprinted 2005

Printed in Grafo, S.A. Basauri

This book is based on *Indiana Jones Explores The Vikings*,
first published in 1994

© text and illustrations
Evans Brothers Limited in this edition 2000

Malam, John
  The Vikings. - (Remains to be seen)
  1.Vikings - Juvenile literature
  I.Title
  948'.022

ISBN 0 237 52597 6

Acknowledgements

The author and publishers would like to thank the following
people for their valuable help and advice:

Dr Anne Millard B.A. (Hons) Dip. ed., Dip. Arc., Ph.D., author,
archaeologist and lecturer

Margaret Sharman author and archaeologist

York Archaeological Trust

Illustrations: Jeffrey Burn page 13
              Virginia Gray pages 12, 21, 29, 33, 38-39
Maps: Jillie Luff, Bitmap Graphics

Editor: Jean Coppendale
Design: Robert and Jean Wheeler Associates
Production: Jenny Mulvanny

For permission to reproduce copyright material the author and
publishers gratefully acknowledge the following:

Cover photograph: Replica of the Oseberg Ship - Robert Harding
Picture Library

Title page: "Sigurd's Helmet" - Werner Forman Archive,
Upplsndsmuseet, Uppsala

page 6 Roger Cracknell, Trip **page 8** Dave Saunders, Trip **page 9**
(left) Robert Harding Picture Library, (right) Icelandic Photo and
Press Service, Mats Wibe Lund **page 10** (top right) Olwen Owen,
Historic Scotland, (middle and bottom right) Universitetets
Oldsaksamling, Oslo **page 11** York Archaeological Trust **page 13**
Icelandic Photo and Press Service, Mats Wibe Lund **page 14** (top
left) York Archaeological Trust, (bottom right) Antiquarian
Topographic Archive, Stockholm, Sweden **page 15** (bottom)
Werener Forman Archive, Statens Historiska Museum, Stockholm,
Sweden, (top) York Archaeological Trust **page 16** York
Archaeological Trust **page 17** (top right) Michael Holford, (top left)
C.M. Dixon, (middle right) Werner Forman Archive, National
Museum, Copenhagen, (bottom left) York Archaeological Trust
page 18 Michael Holford **page 19** (top) Image Select/AKG, (middle
and bottom right) York Archaeological Trust **page 20** (left) C.M.
Dixon, (right) Ronald Sheridan, Ancient Art and Architecture
Collection **page 21** (bottom left) Image Select/AKG (top)
Universitetets Oldsaksamling, Oslo **page 22** (top) Werner Forman
Archive, Viking Ship Museum, Bygdoy, (middle) C.M. Dixon,
(bottom) Image Select/AKG **page 23** Werner Forman Archive,
Statens Historiska Museum, Stockholm, Sweden **page 24** (top left)
Werner Forman Archive, Viking Ship Museum, Bygdoy, (bottom)
Mike Feeney, Trip **page 25** (top) Robert Harding Picture Library,
(bottom) Michael Holford **page 26** (top) C.M. Dixon, (bottom left)
Robert Harding Picture Library, (bottom right) Michael Holford
page 27 (middle) Werner Forman Archive, the British Museum,
(bottom) The Bridgeman Art Library, Giraudon **page 28** (top) York
Archaeological Trust, (bottom) Werner Forman Archive, University
Museum of National Antiquities, Uppsala, Sweden **page 29** York
Archaeological Trust **page 30** Icelandic Photo and Press Service,
Mats Wibe Lund **page 31** Canada Tourist Office **page 32** (bottom
left) C.M. Dixon, (bottom right) Werner Forman Archive, Statens
Historiska Museum, Stockholm, Sweden **page 33** (top left) C.M.
Dixon, (top right) The Bridgeman Art Library, (bottom) Michael
Holford **page 34** York Archaeological Trust **page 35** (top right)
Icelandic Photo and Press Service, Mats Wibe Lund (top left) The
Bridgeman Art Library **page 36** (middle left) York Archaeological
Trust, (bottom right) Robert Harding Picture Library **page 37** (top)
C.M. Dixon, (middle and bottom) York Archaeological Trust **page
39** Antiquarian Topographic Archives, Stockholm, Sweden **page
40** (top left) Michael Holford, (bottom right) Werner Forman
Archive, Statens Historiska Museum, Stockholm, Sweden **page 41**
(top left) George Spencley, Trip, (right) C.M. Dixon **page 42** (top
left) Werner Forman Archive, Thjodminjasafn, Reykjavik, Iceland,
(bottom) C.M. Dixon **page 43** (top left) James D Braund,
Trip, (bottom left) Lesley McIntyre, The Hutchison Library,
(bottom) Michael Holford **page 44** (top) York Archaeological
Trust, (bottom) James D. Braund, Trip **page 45** (top) A.O.C.
(Scotland) Ltd, (bottom) York Archaeological Trust

Contents

TIMELINE OF THE VIKINGS

and the rest of the world

AD **800** — Charlemagne crowned emperor in Rome.

AD **850s** — Mayan culture collapses in Central America.

AD **907** — Last T'ang emperor deposed in China.

1096 — The First Crusade to the Holy Land.

1100s — Toltecs build their capital in Mexico.

AD **800**

AD **900**

AD **1000**

AD **1100**

AD 790s	First Viking raids against England, Scotland and Ireland.
AD 799	First Viking raids against Germany.
AD 800	The Oseberg ship was buried in Norway.
AD 810	First Viking raids against Holland.
AD 835–50	Many Viking raids against England.
AD 839	City of Dublin, Ireland, founded by the Vikings.
AD 839	Swedish Vikings travelled to Russia.
AD 841	Vikings reached Paris, France.
AD 844	First Viking raids against Spain.
AD 850–60	Many Viking raids against France.
AD 860	Norwegian Vikings reached Iceland.
AD 865	Swedish Vikings attacked Constantinople (in present-day Turkey).
AD 865	Viking army from Denmark landed in England.
AD 878	Viking army defeated in England.
AD 885–6	Siege of Paris, France.
AD 886	In England, the Vikings settled in an area of country that became known as the 'Danelaw'.
AD 911	In northern France, the Vikings settled in Normandy.
AD 980s	Christianity spreads throughout the Viking homelands.
AD 982	Eric the Red landed on Greenland.
AD 982	Bjarni Herjulfsson sighted North America, but did not land.
AD 990s	Settlements were built on Greenland.
AD 990s	More Viking raids against England.
1000	Leif Eriksson reached North America.
1010	A small Viking settlement was built in North America at L'Anse aux Meadows (in present-day Canada).
1066	A Norman army invaded England from France and fought the Battle of Hastings. Some of the soldiers were Viking descendants.
1100	The end of the Viking Age.

WHO WERE THE VIKINGS?

Introduction to the Vikings

The Viking Age lasted for about 300 years, from AD 800 to 1100. In this short time the Vikings – or Northmen as they have also been called – achieved many things.

For example, the Vikings were the first people from Europe to reach North America (almost 500 years before Christopher Columbus), and their search for trade and new lands led them to settle in parts of England, Ireland, France, Germany and Russia. They were great sailors and daring adventurers, but they were also bloodthirsty raiders and savage fighters. Modern archaeologists and scholars now know that the Vikings were also traders, settlers and explorers, as well as poets and extremely skilled artists and craftspeople.

This book traces the history and culture of the Vikings. It uses two types of evidence. The main type is evidence from archaeology, which helps us learn about the Vikings by discovering actual remains which have survived from the Viking Age. The other type of evidence comes from written records, made by the Vikings themselves and by other people, too.

Wherever the Vikings travelled to they changed the course of history, and in some places their presence is still felt. They gave many words to the English language, and some towns in England and northern Europe have Viking names.

Fact File

Where did the Vikings come from?

The people we call the Vikings came from a large area in the far north of Europe which today is made up of the countries of Norway, Sweden and Denmark. Together with Finland the geographical name for this area is Scandinavia.

Today, Norway, Sweden and Denmark are separate countries. Each has its own distinctive language and culture. It was during the Viking Age that these lands first began to emerge as individual countries, even though the people who lived there had many things in common. They spoke a similar language, built similar houses and sailed in similar types of ship. Probably the most important thing they had in common was being close to the sea. Most Viking settlements were built along the coast and in order to reach other villages the Vikings had to be expert sailors. In time they mastered the sea and travelled further than any Europeans had ever done before.

The lands the Vikings came from each have distinctive landscapes. Norway is mountainous with expanses of pine and birch forest and many deep inlets of narrow water lead into the sea. The Norwegian word for these inlets is 'fjord'. Sweden has mountains too, but also areas of fertile, lower-lying land. Denmark is almost flat – its highest hill is only 179 metres high.

The Viking World

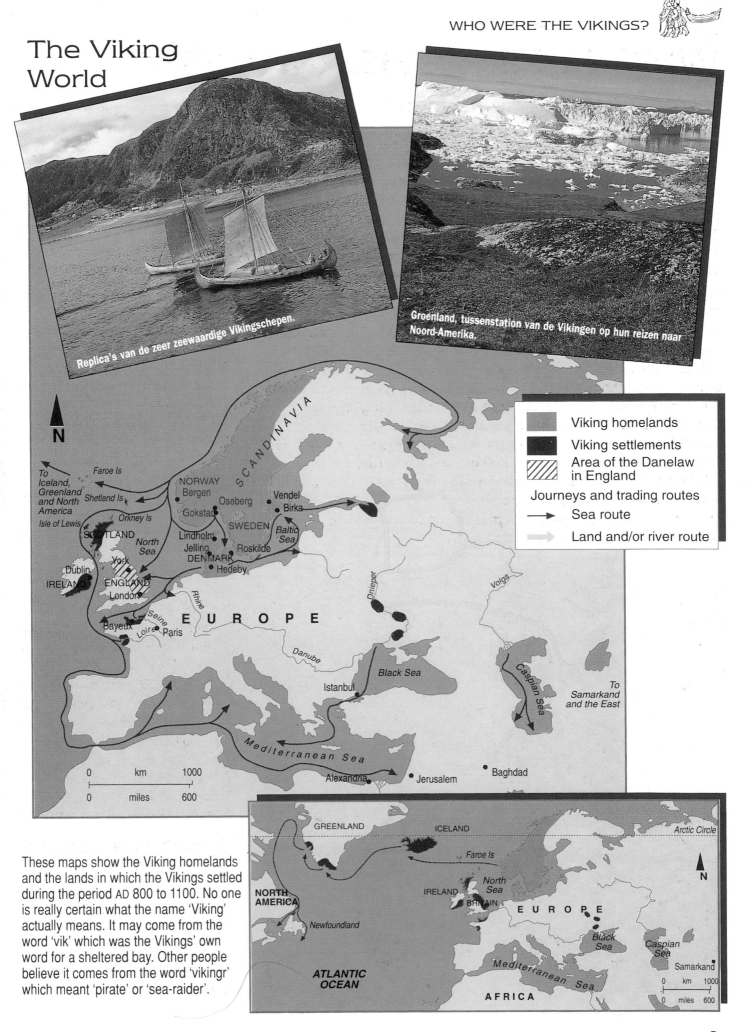

Replica's van de zeer zeewaardige Vikingschepen.

Groenland, tussenstation van de Vikingen op hun reizen naar Noord-Amerika.

Legend

	Viking homelands
	Viking settlements
	Area of the Danelaw in England

Journeys and trading routes

→ Sea route

→ Land and/or river route

These maps show the Viking homelands and the lands in which the Vikings settled during the period AD 800 to 1100. No one is really certain what the name 'Viking' actually means. It may come from the word 'vik' which was the Vikings' own word for a sheltered bay. Other people believe it comes from the word 'vikingr' which meant 'pirate' or 'sea-raider'.

WORLD OF THE VIKINGS

Everyday life

Did you know that archaeologists have a lot in common with detectives? They both look for clues that will solve problems and find answers. The clues that archaeologists look for are the bits and pieces left behind by people who died long ago. After they've been found, only then can archaeologists start to build up a picture of what people's lives might have been like long ago. Archaeology is not about guessing what life was like in the past – it's about finding actual remains and understanding them.

What was left behind by the Vikings? Thanks to rubbish thrown out by Viking craftspeople, we know that Viking towns were busy places with lots going on. Some streets were industrial, where all kinds of different products were made. Wood-workers made furniture and kitchen utensils. Blacksmiths shaped iron into tools and weapons. Potters worked clay into cooking pots. Bone-workers took animal bones and antlers from the butchers' to cut into combs, gaming dice and ice skates. Leather-workers used animal skins from the slaughter-houses and set about their smelly and unpleasant work of turning them into leather for shoes, clothes and containers such as buckets and jugs.

A small plaque made from whalebone decorated with horses' heads. It was an ironing board used for pressing seams in clothes. It may have been a wedding gift from a husband to his wife. It was made in Norway and was found with the bodies of a Viking family buried on Orkney, Scotland.

Sledges such as this were probably an important method of transport over snow and ice. This wooden sledge was found buried with the Oseberg ship (see page 23).

This wooden wagon was found buried with the Oseberg ship (see page 23). From this unique example we can find out about the kind of wheeled transport the Vikings used on land.

Fact File

Food and drink

Vikings ate their meals in the main room of the house. They sat on the floor, on long benches or on fold-away chairs. Food was cooked over an open fire in a cooking pot that was often suspended from the rafters. The food was served on wooden bowls and dishes. Fish and shellfish were very popular. Meat was also eaten, either cooked with vegetables such as cabbages and onions in a stew or roasted separately. Meat came from farm animals (such as cows, sheep and chickens) and from hunting.

Vikings who lived in the far north hunted polar bears and reindeer, while those in the south trapped hares and wild boars. Bread and porridge were made from cereals, and butter and cheese were made from milk. Food was seasoned with sea salt and with spices (such as pepper) brought back by travellers. The Vikings did not know about sugar, so honey was used as a sweetener both for food and drink. Beer made from hops was a common drink. At sea, pre-cooked food was eaten cold. It was too dangerous to heat it over a fire. Salted fish and dried meat were eaten on long sea voyages.

Life in the country was quieter. People lived off produce they grew or caught for themselves. Coastal villagers looked after boats, mended nets and processed the day's catch of fish. Inland, villagers tilled the soil and tended farm animals. Weavers, usually women, worked on looms inside the long-houses, making cloth for garments.

Archaeologists know that spinning and weaving was women's work because objects used in the making of cloth are found in their graves, and not in the graves of men. And, at the end of the day, board games were played for fun and relaxation (see page 19).

▲ Two wooden spoons. Although their handles have not survived, you can still see how similar they are to wooden spoons used today.

Combs were made from animal bones or antlers. Some were decorated with carved designs. This comb was found together with its case. ▼

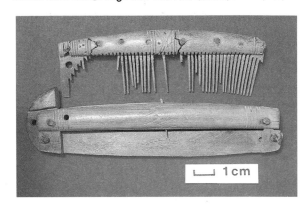

1 cm

No part of an animal was wasted. Its meat was cooked and eaten, its skin became leather and even bones from its skeleton were useful. Attached to the bottom of this leather shoe is a bone which acted as a skate for use when crossing ice.

Inside a Viking long-house

What was a Viking house like? Most Vikings lived in small farming settlements in the country or along the coast. Their houses were long, low and narrow and are often called 'long-houses'. By the end of the Viking Age houses were built with smaller rooms attached to the main long room.

Viking houses were made from timber, turf or stone. Turf was easy to cut and stack and it gave good protection from the cold. A turf house could last for about 25 years before it was time to knock it down and build a new one.

Houses at the start of the Viking Age did not have windows, and their insides were dark and gloomy. Towards the end of the Viking Age some houses had simple windows made from see-through animal bladders stretched across holes in the walls. In the centre of the room was the hearth, with a fire burning directly on the earth floor. The fire gave heat and light. It was important to burn the correct type of fuel, otherwise smoke would quickly fill the house. An opening cut in the roof let the smoke escape. The roof was made from thatch or wooden tiles and there was always a risk it would catch fire.

A Viking house had little furniture. Low benches of beaten earth along the walls were for sitting on and for storing the family's possessions. Beds were laid out at night, and put away each morning.

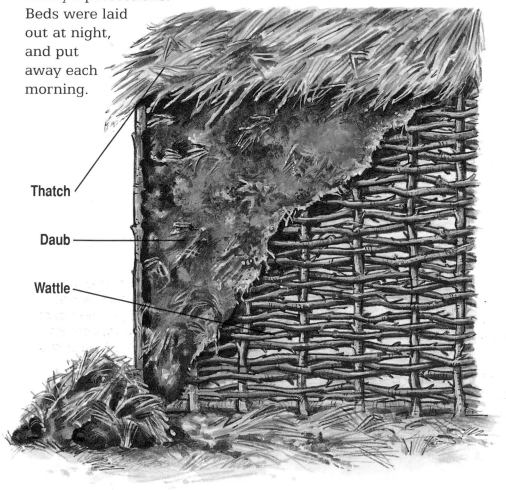

Thatch

Daub

Wattle

Fact File

Wattle and daub

Town houses were smaller than country long-houses and they were often made entirely of wood. Strong houses were built of oak planks and posts held together with wooden pegs called 'treenails'. Other houses were built from rows of thin hazel or willow twigs, carefully knitted between sturdy upright wooden stakes. The result was a woven network of tightly packed twigs called a 'wattle'. Several wattles were then joined together to form the basic shape of the new house which looked like a large basket at this stage. The wattle framework was flimsy and full of gaps, so the wattles were daubed with a thick mixture of clay, straw and animal manure. After setting hard, a wattle and daub house could be painted both outside and inside with a wash of white lime. Patch repairs were carried out by filling holes with extra daub. If looked after the house would last for many years.

Wattle and daub has been used for thousands of years and as recently as 100 years ago in some parts of Europe.

▲ A Viking family inside a long-house built in one of the Viking homelands. Note the central hearth, the low benches, the earth floor, the weaving loom, the wall-hangings, and the lack of windows and furniture.

Conditions were both cramped and smelly inside a Viking long-house. You'd have to get on well with the rest of your family, and with visitors who came to stay! Everyone lived, slept and even worked in that one long room. In the winter farm animals might be kept at one end of the house. This helped to keep the animals alive, but it was also an early form of 'central heating', since the warmth from the animals' bodies would heat the house – and keep the Vikings cosy!

Towns and ports

Archaeologists uncovering the Viking town of Jorvik (York) in the 1970s. Their excavation was in a street called Coppergate which meant 'street of the wood-workers' in the Viking language. Remains of a Viking wood-working industry, from which the street name was derived, were found.

The Vikings did not build towns out of stone. If they had, the chances are that we'd be able to walk along preserved Viking streets and look inside ancient buildings – just like the towns built by the Ancient Greeks and the Romans. But no such luck with the Vikings. Their towns were made of perishable materials such as wood and thatch, which if they hadn't burnt down had long since disappeared under later buildings put up over them. It is only through the work of archaeologists, who have uncovered parts of Viking towns in Norway, Sweden, Denmark, England, Ireland and Germany, that we know anything about these ancient settlements at all.

Jorvik: a Viking town in England

Jorvik (pronounced 'yor-vik'), or York as we call the town today, is the best-known Viking town in England. Vikings settled there in the 870s and established a busy town second only in size and importance to London. They built narrow, winding streets lined with small wooden houses and workshops. The River Ouse flowed through the town to the North Sea. It was along this highway that their boats sailed to reach other parts of the Viking world. Objects such as amber from Denmark, shells from the Red Sea and coins from Asia were all brought to Jorvik by Viking travellers.

Birka: a Viking port in Sweden

Built on a Swedish island, Birka was a busy international port and trading centre. Boats brought goods from all over the world to Birka – silk from China, jewellery from Asia, glass and pottery from Germany. People of many different nationalities would have gone to Birka to buy and trade goods.

The Viking port of Birka, Sweden, is buried beneath the turf of these fields. The uneven lumps and bumps in the fields are the hidden remains of the town which was surrounded by a defensive bank of soil.

Metal tools used by Jorvik's Viking wood-workers for shaping, splitting and drilling wood.

Fact File

Unearthing the Vikings of Jorvik

How useful is archaeology? If you visit the city of York in the north of England then you'll see just how much archaeologists can discover by digging into the ground. One excavation in particular has done more than any others to bring the lost world of the Vikings back to life. In 1976 archaeologists began to excavate a site in York city centre, in a street known as Coppergate. This street was chosen because its name meant 'street of the wood-workers' in the Viking language, and this was a clue that Vikings may once have been there. The archaeologists dug deep into the ground and discovered well-preserved remains dating to the Viking Age – they belonged to the town the Vikings called Jorvik. Floors and walls from wooden buildings were found together with over 15,000 objects which help us to understand what life was like in a Viking town in England just over 1,000 years ago. Today there is a visitors' centre built on the site where you can see some of the discoveries the archaeologists made (see page 44).

Hedeby: a Viking town in Denmark

Hedeby was one of the largest Viking towns. Like the port of Birka, it too was a trading centre. It had well-built wooden houses that faced on to streets which were covered with wooden planks. The wooden houses were probably the homes of wealthy traders. Poorer people lived in small houses built from wattle and daub (see page 12). Their houses faced on to wet and muddy alleys.

These silver coins were found in the Viking port of Birka, Sweden. They were probably minted at Hedeby, Denmark, and used to buy goods in Birka's important market. One shows a longship, the other an animal. The Vikings were the first people in Scandinavia to use coins.

Clothing and jewellery

What we know about Viking clothes is almost entirely based on fragments found on excavations – and it's a wonder that even these have survived because organic materials usually decay quickly. Wool, linen, leather and fur were the chief materials used to make Viking clothes.

For everyday wear, women wore long woollen dresses with embroidered patterns and colourful designs. Worn over the dresses were large rectangular pieces of cloth. One hung down the front of the body, the other down the back. Large oval brooches held the pieces in place, attaching them at the shoulders. They covered their hair with a scarf.

Viking men wore woollen tunics and trousers. The tunics were knee-length. A leather belt around the waist kept their trousers up and their tunics were tucked under it.

For outdoor clothing, woollen or fur cloaks were worn by both men and women. Woollen socks and leather boots or shoes were also worn by men and women, and men wore leather or fur caps.

Wealthy Vikings, and those in the nobility, had expensive clothes made from materials such as imported silk from China. Elaborate patterns woven from fine gold and silver thread decorated dresses and tunics. Viking travellers who had been to the east returned wearing baggy trousers – copied from the ones worn by Arabs (see page 29). Children dressed like their parents, but girls kept their heads uncovered, except in very cold weather.

Fact File

Jewellery

The Vikings wore many different pieces of jewellery. Gold, silver and bronze bracelets and rings that fastened around the neck were popular as were brooches. Surprisingly, finger rings were seldom worn. Strings of beads were made from glass, jet (a black stone), and amber (a fossilized resin from pine trees). Jewellery was a sign of personal wealth, and both men and women could show how rich they were by the gold and silver they wore. Viking jewellery was often made from gold and silver coins brought back from expeditions overseas, especially to the Arab countries of the east and to England in the west. The coins were either melted down or kept intact and strung together. Debts could be paid for with jewellery and when this happened the people settling the debt had to agree on how much a piece of jewellery was worth to them. If it was worth more than the debt, then it could be cut up to an agreed value – and what was left could be made into a new, smaller, piece of jewellery.

A leather shoe found in the Viking town of Jorvik, England. It has a flat sole and was fastened with a leather thong. Next to it is the wooden block (called a 'last') that was used by the cobbler to make the shoe.

A Viking woman's jewellery. The large oval brooches made of decorated bronze pinned her clothes at her shoulders. The beads are of cornelian (a red stone), glass and rock crystal. The small brooch in the centre has a loop through it and it may have been worn around the neck on a chain. ▶

A dress fastener such as this had two functions – it was a decorative piece of jewellery and it pinned clothes together. We know it was worn on the shoulder from the position it was found in when a Viking grave was excavated.

Hairstyles

Viking people kept their hair long – even men. Women usually wore their hair tied back or in a plait. Men grew beards and moustaches. Both men and women carried combs made from animal bone (see page 11), and they spent time cleaning and combing their hair.

Gold brooches with elaborate designs. Only a very wealthy Viking could afford jewellery of this quality.

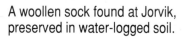

A woollen sock found at Jorvik, preserved in water-logged soil.

Art, entertainment and music

The Vikings were skilled artists. They used intricate patterns to decorate a wide variety of objects, such as ships, tombstones, bone combs, weapons and jewellery. No matter where the Vikings settled in Scandinavia and Europe, the same patterns were used by their artists time and time again. By recognizing the Viking styles of art, archaeologists can tell the difference between Vikings and other people who lived at the same time as they did in Europe, such as Saxons in England, Frisians in Holland and Franks in Germany.

One style of art used intertwining animals to create extraordinary twisted patterns. At first sight you may not see the animals at all – until you spot a head and then a leg and then a body. Other patterns were simpler, formed from geometric shapes such as squares, triangles and lines.

In very rare circumstances pieces of embroidered cloth have survived, such as a large fragment found entombed with the Oseberg ship (see pages 21 and 23). Wealthy Vikings used decorated cloths to adorn the insides of their houses, lining the walls with strips of brightly coloured fabric.

◀ A tombstone found in St Paul's Cathedral churchyard, London. The carving is a large animal entwined by a smaller snake-like creature. An inscription says, 'Ginna and Toki had this stone set up'. It has been painted the same colours it was originally painted in, 950 years ago.

Chess may have been played by the Vikings, who could have seen it in countries in the east where the game began. These ivory figures were found on the Isle of Lewis, Scotland, in 1831. They date from the very end of the Viking Age and seem to represent a knight, a queen and a bishop.

A good example of Viking art where many animals have been so twisted together that only their heads can be seen at first. This is part of a church doorway from Norway.

In the game of 'hnefatafl' the object was to surround an opponent's king. Counters from this game, usually made from glass, are often found in Viking graves but so far a complete set has not been found – so we don't know how many pieces each player had.

How did the Vikings entertain themselves? Apart from telling stories called 'sagas' (see page 20), the Vikings played board games. Ivory figures found in Scotland suggest they played a game like chess, though this was not widespread. More common was the game of 'hnefatafl', a game played with counters.

Games of strength were also played. Wrestlers grappled with each other to the point of exhaustion when one man was forced to give in. In another game, strongmen carried boulders as far as they could without dropping them. One sport that died out with the Vikings was horse-fighting, where horses bit and kicked each other.

Fact File

Music and singing

How can we tell what Viking music was like? Evidence of music is difficult to find. An Arab trader called Al-Tattushi gives us a clue about how musical the Vikings were. He wrote, 'I have not heard a more horrible singing. It is like a growl coming out of their throats, like dogs barking, only much more beastly.' Is this a fair description? Probably not. Viking singing would have sounded strange to Al-Tattushi – as it would do to us too. Sadly, we have no evidence of Viking songs, because their songs were passed on by mouth and not written down. We are a little luckier when it comes to Viking musical instruments, for fragments of pipes, like the so-called 'Pipes of Pan' have been found as have pieces of stringed instruments, similar to harps. No doubt the Vikings had other wind, percussion and string instruments too – but so far none have been found.

Part of a Viking 'Pipes of Pan'. Four notes can still be played, by blowing across the holes.

Viking sagas and writing

Sagas were stories composed by the Vikings, some of which have survived to the present day. From them we can learn about Viking life, famous Vikings, places the Vikings visited and many other details that an archaeologist would never discover by excavation alone. For example, we knew the Vikings had reached North America long before archaeologists found remains of a Viking settlement there, because the discovery was told in Viking sagas.

Sagas were passed on by word of mouth. But some were written down by monks living on Iceland in the 1200s, after the Viking Age had ended, and these are the ones we know today. There must have been many more sagas that told stories of bravery and adventure, but as they were never written down they were forgotten and are now lost. Skilled story-tellers memorized the sagas and could recite them in full. Njal's Saga was the most famous Viking saga. It tells of a conflict between the forces of good and evil as seen through the lives of ordinary people.

Viking poets, who were known as 'skalds', recited poems. Some had hundreds of verses. The 'skalds' used made-up names for objects instead of using the object's real name. The listener had to decide for himself what the poet was really talking about! These names are called 'kennings'. For example, there were several 'kennings' that all meant a longship, such as 'oar-steed', 'horse of the sea', 'fjord-elk' or 'surf-dragon'. In each case the idea was to create a new way of thinking about a longship, making the poem more powerful to the listener.

Viking graffiti? This inscription is carved in runes inside Maes Howe prehistoric tomb on the mainland island of Orkney, Scotland. There are several inscriptions inside the tomb, carved about 1150. They refer to a 'great treasure' hidden nearby, but nothing is known of this.

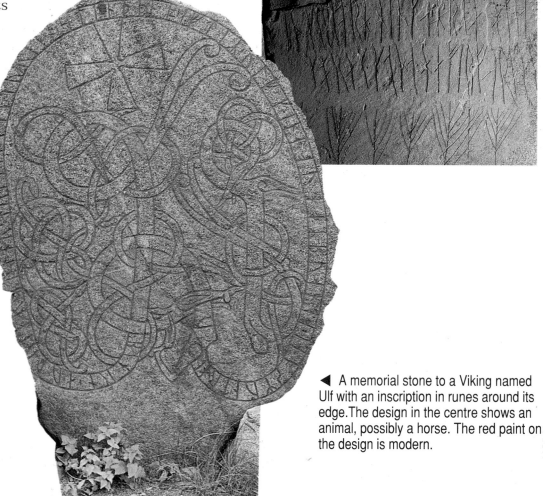

◄ A memorial stone to a Viking named Ulf with an inscription in runes around its edge. The design in the centre shows an animal, possibly a horse. The red paint on the design is modern.

The rare fragment of tapestry on the right was found buried with the Oseberg ship (see page 23). It shows a procession of horse-drawn wagons and soldiers. The pictures may be part of a Viking saga, though which one is not known. The picture above is an artist's reconstruction of how the pattern may have looked.

◀ The story of the hero Sigurd is told in a series of wooden carvings from a church in Norway. In this scene he kills a dragon before taking its gold.

Fact File

Runes – the Viking alphabet

Some Vikings, though probably not all, could read and write. They created a system of writing where each letter was made from a series of short straight lines which were easy to carve on hard surfaces. It would have been much harder to carve the letters if they had been curved. The individual letters are called 'runes', which some people think comes from a word meaning 'to whisper'. The script to which they belong is called the 'futhark', which is the Viking equivalent of 'alphabet'. Just as that word is formed from 'alpha' and 'beta' (Greek for a and b), so 'futhark' is formed by the first six letters of the Viking script. Runes were not invented by the Vikings. They adapted a script already in use in some parts of central Europe. At first the Viking 'futhark' had 24 letters, but this was reduced to 16 by AD 800. Runes were gradually replaced by the Latin alphabet as the Vikings were converted to Christianity (see page 43).

▼ The 16 runes of the Viking alphabet.

VOYAGES AND DISCOVERIES

Longships and merchant ships

The prow of a Viking longship was carved with a dragon's head which gave it the name 'dragon ship'. This dragon was found with the Oseberg ship, carved on a wooden post, its use is unknown.

Norway, Sweden and Denmark have long coastlines, and in the Viking Age sea travel was the quickest way to get around (see the map on page 9). We know about Viking ships because some have been found inside burial mounds and also at the bottom of lakes. There are many examples of preserved Viking ships in museums in Denmark and Norway.

How did Viking ships develop? We believe the ancestors of all Viking ships were long, narrow rowing boats used in prehistoric times, hundreds of years before the Viking Age. We know how these vessels looked from rock carvings, from which we can tell they were for coastal sailing only – they would have capsized on the open sea.

Together with improvements for shaping and joining wood, other advances in ship technology were made by the Vikings. They added masts, sails, rudders for steering and keels for stability at sea (a keel is a ship's backbone, running its length under the hull). These advances meant that Viking ships could sail further and faster than ships had done before.

Prehistoric rock carvings from Denmark showing two rowing boats – the ancestors of the fearsome Viking longships. They date from about 1000 BC.

The excavation of a 1,200-year-old Viking ship, found at Oseberg, Norway, as photographed in 1904. The Oseberg ship was 22 metres long. When not under sail, it would have been rowed by a crew of 30 oarsmen. Wooden oars were found buried with the ship. From its shape it seems it was sailed in calm coastal water and not on the rough open sea.

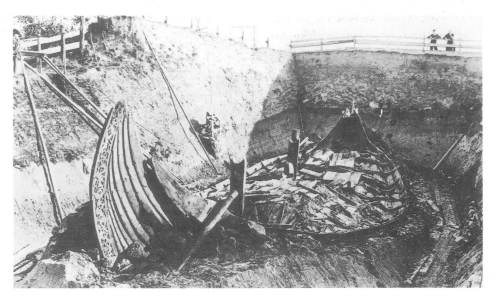

Fact File

The Oseberg ship

In August 1903 news reached the University of Oslo, Norway, of an exciting discovery. At Oseberg, a town about 70 kilometres south of Oslo, workmen had dug into a large mound and found a ship buried beneath air-tight layers of clay and peat. When the mound was excavated the following year, archaeologists unearthed a well-preserved Viking ship made of oak. Today we call it the 'Oseberg ship'. It is about 1,200 years old and was buried about AD 800. The weight of the mound above the ship had slowly crushed it into over 3,000 pieces. Each piece was numbered and after treatment to prevent them from decaying the pieces were joined back together.

Why was the ship buried? Archaeologists discovered it held the remains of two women – one aged about 60 and the other about 25. No one knows who they were, except that they were wealthy and probably important people. They had been buried with some remarkable objects including a four-wheeled wagon, sledges, beds, chairs, a weaving loom, textiles and personal possessions. Sadly, robbers had broken into the burial chamber long ago and had taken the valuable jewellery and ornaments that were probably buried with the mysterious Viking women.

A metal weather-vane from the mast or prow of a longship. Colourful streamers may have been tied to the holes around the edge.

Longships

The supreme Viking ship was the longship or 'drakkar' – often called a 'dragon ship' because of its prow which was decorated with a carving of a dragon's head. It was a fast vessel and was used by raiders. It was up to 25 metres long and at sea was powered by a large rectangular woollen sail. Oarsmen rowed the ship when it was in coastal or inland waters. A longship had a flat bottom which meant it could sail in shallow water, such as a river. It was light for its size, and when exploring new lands the crew could haul it overland to the next river.

Merchant ships

These ships, called 'knörr', were sturdier than longships. They needed to be, since their job was to carry passengers, animals and supplies. Life on a merchant ship was hard. There were no cabins and everyone had to stay on the open deck, even in bad weather.

This drawing shows a group of Viking soldiers carrying a small boat overland. Inside the boat are the soldiers' weapons. The drawing was made in the 1500s. Carrying a full-size ship this way would have been impossible. Instead, it may have been dragged on wooden rollers.

Why did the Vikings cross the sea?

What came first, the perfect ship for crossing the rough seas around Norway, Sweden and Denmark, or the Viking will to search for new lands? There's no easy answer to this, except to say the two are closely linked. We know there were good sailing ships from the very start of the Viking Age, from about AD 800. This was also the time the Vikings sailed from their homelands to start new settlements, to trade for goods they didn't have at home, and to plunder valuable goods from the lands they reached.

Two important factors seem to have caused the Vikings to cross the sea. First, good farming land was in short supply at home. The sea level was higher then than it is today, so there was less farming land to go around. Second, we now believe the early Vikings suffered a population explosion. Add these two points together, and the Vikings must have realized they had to search out new lands to support their growing population - and with their ocean-going ships they had the means to do this.

In recent times, full-scale replicas (copies) of Viking ships have been made. By doing this it has been possible to learn about the skills the Vikings had, as ship-builders and as sailors. These modern craft have sailed on the open sea, and their crews have used the same methods of navigation that the Vikings did. This process is called experimental archaeology. It is a way of finding out about the past by doing experiments.

This ship was found in 1880 at Gokstad in Norway. It dates from about AD 850. A full-scale replica of this ship crossed the Atlantic Ocean from Bergen, Norway, to Newfoundland, Canada in 1893. The crossing took only 28 days.

In the 1960s five Viking ships were found at the bottom of the fjord at Roskilde, Denmark. They had been loaded with stones and deliberately sunk to form a barrier against attackers. There were two longships in the group of the kind that were probably used on raids.

Fact File

Navigation

Imagine sailing out of sight of land: how would you know where you were? And how would you know where you were heading? These were problems faced by all Viking sailors – so being able to navigate well was an important skill to master. Making a mistake could lead to the loss of the ship and all on board.

The skilled navigator knew how to judge distances and directions from landmarks, sea birds and fish he saw. He knew from experience which species lived close to land, and which did not. He used the positions of the sun and the Pole Star to calculate how far north or south he was sailing. On days when the sun wasn't visible he may have used a 'sun stone' to work out the sun's position. This was a piece of Iceland spar-stone which changed colour from yellow to pale blue when pointed in the direction of the hidden sun. Learning from other navigators was important too, and passing information between each other helped the Vikings understand the seas they sailed. They may have kept maps and charts – but we know very little about this side of Viking navigation.

A replica of a merchant ship called a 'knörr'. Ships such as this were used for long-distance travel and trade. A ship of this type was found in the Roskilde fjord, Denmark.

The Bayeux Tapestry is a long, embroidered piece of cloth made to celebrate the successful invasion of England by Norman soldiers in 1066. This part shows the building of ships that resemble Viking longships. The Normans had Viking connections.

Viking raiders: western Europe

The skill and courage of the Vikings took them to countries throughout western Europe. The effects of their raids were great and for countries such as England and France the Vikings changed the course of history.

England, Scotland and Ireland

The first Vikings in England came from Norway and arrived in the AD 790s. They were not friendly visitors but had come to raid and pillage. They attacked towns and villages along the east coast, and then sailed home with their plunder. There were few raids at first, but in AD 865 a Viking army from Denmark landed in East Anglia with plans to capture land and valuables. Within 30 years of their landing, much of northern and eastern England was under Viking rule. This area became known as the 'Danelaw', where Viking customs were observed and where the official language was Norse.

   Northern Scotland and Ireland were attacked and settled by Vikings from Norway. They established control here as well as in the Isle of Man and parts of western England. Their base was in Ireland, on the banks of the River Liffey where today the capital city Dublin stands.

Lindisfarne monastery, on Holy Island, off the coast of north-east England, was the subject of several raids from Vikings in their search for valuables.

A hoard of silver jewellery looted by Vikings, chopped up and buried for recovery later. Silver from hoards such as this is called 'hack silver' because of the way it has been roughly hacked up to make it easier to carry and then melt down. ▼

◄ At Lerwick, capital of the Shetland Islands, the fire festival of Up-Hella-Aa is held each January to mark the beginning of the new year. A replica longship is set alight. It is a modern festival and was created to remember the islands' Viking past.

Fact File

Danegeld

Apart from capturing land and stealing valuables, the Vikings also collected a tax called the 'Danegeld'. This meant 'Danes' gold', and it was the price paid for peace. The Vikings demanded gold, silver and other valuables and if they didn't get what they wanted, then towns and villages would be destroyed and people taken into slavery. Large amounts of 'Danegeld' were paid. More than 330,000 kilograms of silver were paid by the English in the 23 years between AD 991 and 1014. Coins, jewellery, plates, bowls, cups and church silver were gathered up and taken across the North Sea to be melted down in the Viking homelands. If you're interested in early-English silver coins, then a good place to see some is in Denmark, where more have been found than in England – no doubt paid as 'Danegeld' by the Anglo-Saxons and taken to Denmark by the Vikings.

France

At the same time as a Viking army was conquering parts of England, one from Denmark was making progress in France. Viking soldiers besieged the city of Paris in AD 885 and captured land in the north of the country. In AD 911 the French king made a treaty with the Viking leader, Rollo. In return for Rollo becoming a Christian and ending Viking raids against French towns, he was given land in an area called 'Northmannia', a name that meant the 'land of the Northmen'. Today we call this area of northern France Normandy. Rollo's soldiers became landowners and it was their Norman descendants who in 1066 invaded England and defeated the Saxon king Harold Godwinson at the Battle of Hastings.

▲ Silver coins made for Viking rulers in England. They may have been minted from silver collected from the English which was a tax known as 'Danegeld'.

Boats of the Norman fleet crossing the English Channel from France in 1066. The Norman soldiers were descended from Vikings. Note the similarities between their boats and Viking longships. This is a scene on the Bayeux Tapestry. ▼

Viking traders: eastern Europe and Asia

Can you imagine what it must have been like to witness a Viking raid? After an attack on the Lindisfarne monastry in AD 793, one of the monks described the Vikings as, 'stinging hornets', and ' ... like terrible wolves'. But the Vikings who set sail from Sweden had a very different plan from those that sailed from Denmark and Norway. Unlike Danish and Norwegian Vikings who sent raiding parties to the shores of western Europe, Vikings from Sweden were more interested in trading with people who lived in eastern Europe and as far away as Asia.

This cowrie shell was found in Jorvik, England. It had been taken there from the Red Sea, and is a sign of long-distance trade.

Russia

The Swedish Vikings had a powerful influence on the early history of Russia. It is said that in AD 862 an invitation was sent to them by the Slav people who lived in Russia. It said: 'Our country is rich and immense, but is rent by disorder. Come and govern us and reign over us'. The Slavs hoped the Vikings would settle in Russia and bring peace to the warring tribes in their land – which they did. The Slavs called these Vikings the 'Rus'. It was the 'Rus' who gave their name to Russia.

The great rivers of Russia flow from north to south in the northern part of the land, and in the southern part they flow from south to north. The Vikings sailed up and down the rivers and established trading centres along them. The inter-connecting river system opened up the vast interior of Russia. Here Viking traders found rich goods, such as animal furs. Goods were collected and taken back to Viking towns such as Birka and Hedeby (see page 15).

Asia

Some of the most expensive (and desirable) goods were found in the distant lands of Asia. They came within reach of Viking traders once they had established their trading network along the Russian rivers. Silk from China was one of the most luxurious goods in demand by wealthy Vikings. The Vikings never actually reached China. But Viking merchants probably traded with Arabs who were in contact with the Chinese. This meant the Vikings could buy silk and other exotic goods such as spices, from most parts of the known world.

Imagine the many hands a length of delicate silk must have passed through before it finally reached its destination in Scandinavia – and imagine the excitement of seeing and handling such a rare item.

Fact File

The slave trade

There was an unpleasant side to Viking trade – the taking of slaves. People were a commodity to be traded just as silver and furs were. In Scandinavia slavery was a punishment for committing certain crimes. Slaves worked for a master and did hard-labour jobs. Slaves taken on raids against Christian lands in western Europe were held for ransom from the Christian church. Christians were against slavery. They saw it as a pagan practice. Many slaves were taken in eastern Europe. These people were transported thousands of kilometres along Viking trade routes and were sold to Arabs at slave markets from where they were taken to North Africa and Spain. The Viking towns of Hedeby and Birka also saw slaves pass through their markets, on their way to uncertain futures.

◀ A pair of merchant's travelling scales.

▲ An Arab coin found in Jorvik, England. It was minted in the town of Samarkand, on the edge of the Himalayas – some 4,500 kilometres from Jorvik.

A Viking couple buying goods from a merchant who has been to the furthest parts of the Viking world. He has returned with rare spices and luxurious silks. Using a small pair of travelling scales, he checks the weight of the couple's gold. In return he sells them the goods. Note their clothes. The merchant's baggy trousers are copied from ones worn by Arabs. Gold threads decorate the edges of his tunic, and fur lines his hat. Large shoulder brooches fasten rectangles of material to the woman's linen tunic. A small pair of clippers hangs from one brooch. Her husband's woollen cloak is draped over his left shoulder, leaving his sword-arm (right arm) free to fight with.

VIKING PEOPLE

Leaders, soldiers and the army

Fact File

Law and government

What was Viking law like? And what about Viking government – how were people ruled? It's important to remember that the Vikings did not have one overall capital city from which to organize a government throughout their lands. Instead, each town and village organized its own local rule – but they all followed a similar style no matter where they were in the Viking world. An open-air meeting called a 'Thing' was held in towns and villages twice a year. It lasted several days and was made up of all the free men in the area. Women, children and slaves could not attend. Taxes were set and quarrels were settled at these important meetings.

Vikings on the Isle of Man held their meetings, called 'Things' at this spot. Today it is called Tynwald Hill which means 'Thing Plain Hill'. Tynwald is also the name of the Isle of Man parliament – from the Viking word 'Thing'.

Who ruled the Vikings? The Viking countries were never united under one ruler. Several separate Viking kingdoms existed at the same time and each one had its own chief or king. The king had to be a strong leader who could raise and command an army and keep law and order in his kingdom. He was also seen as head of the Viking religion and, in pre-Christian times, he claimed to be descended from a god. When the king died, power was passed to one of his relations - usually his brother, son or a nephew. Viking women could never become rulers. Sometimes power was shared between relatives who divided the old kingdom into smaller parts.

The king appointed officials called 'earls' to look after the day-to-day running of his kingdom. These men were wealthy high ranking nobles. It was their work to collect taxes from the ordinary people and in times of unrest to summon them to join the army.

The army

Under Viking law adult men were expected to serve in the army if the need arose. The Vikings did not have one big army. Instead, each kingdom had its own small force of soldiers whose main job was to protect the king.

The bravest Viking soldiers were called 'berserkers'. It is said that before a battle they howled like wolves, and bit on the edges of their shields. They worked themselves up into a frenzy, and many went into battle bare-chested. If they were injured, they were supposed not to feel any pain. Our own expression 'to go berserk' comes from the name of these brave warriors.

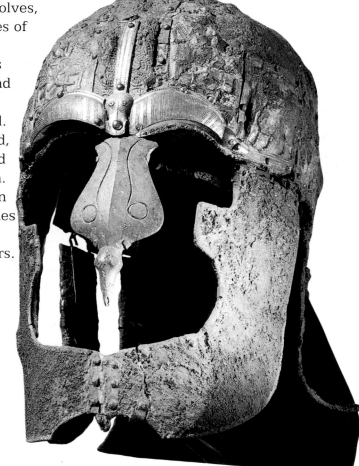

A helmet made from bronze and iron. The cheek, neck and nose guards gave good all-round protection. It was found at Vendel, Sweden and dates from the very beginning of the Viking period.

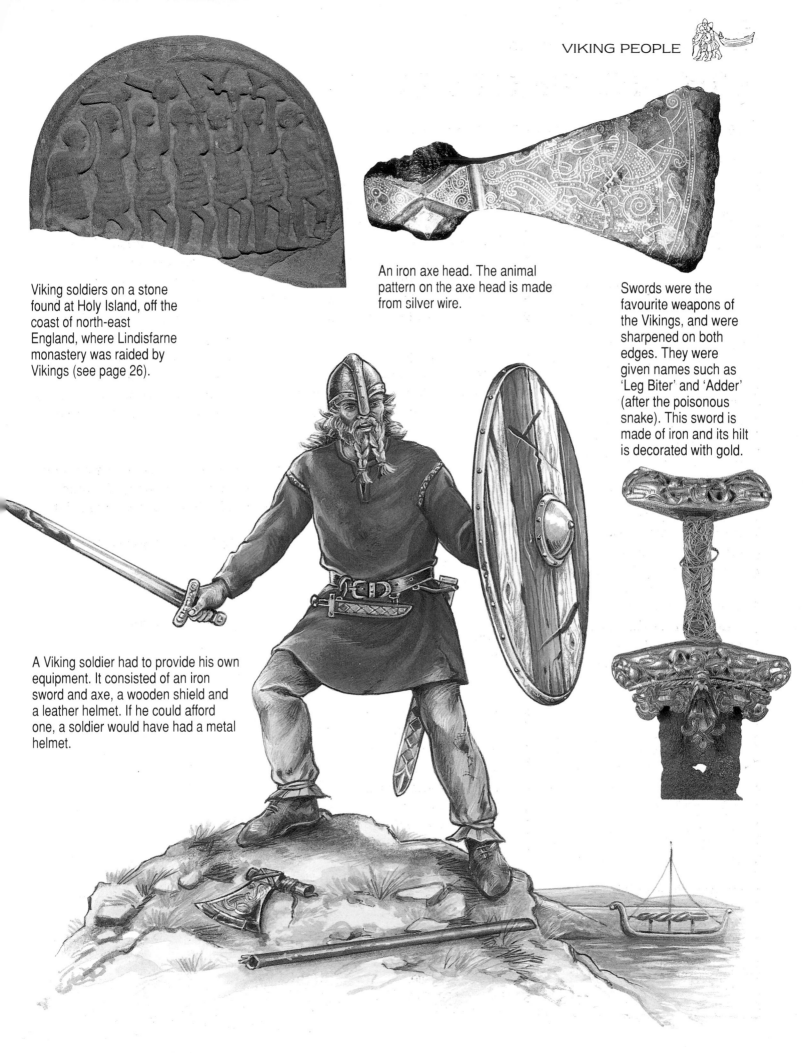

Viking soldiers on a stone found at Holy Island, off the coast of north-east England, where Lindisfarne monastery was raided by Vikings (see page 26).

An iron axe head. The animal pattern on the axe head is made from silver wire.

Swords were the favourite weapons of the Vikings, and were sharpened on both edges. They were given names such as 'Leg Biter' and 'Adder' (after the poisonous snake). This sword is made of iron and its hilt is decorated with gold.

A Viking soldier had to provide his own equipment. It consisted of an iron sword and axe, a wooden shield and a leather helmet. If he could afford one, a soldier would have had a metal helmet.

Three famous Vikings

We know about many individual Vikings, particularly those who became great warriors or explorers. The Vikings told stories (sagas) about them, and it is these sources that help us piece together the events of their lives.

Eric the Red

Eric Thorwaldsson (called Eric the Red because of his red hair) was born in Norway about AD 950. In AD 982 he was accused of murder and sent away from Iceland, where he had been living, for three years. Eric and his followers sailed west from Iceland to search for a new land. He sailed to a land first seen by a Viking adventurer 50 years before. On return to Iceland, Eric told people about the country he had sailed to. It had fertile green valleys and he called it 'Greenland' – the name we use today. He took a group of people to Greenland where they built settlements. Eric died on Greenland in about 1010.

Leif Eriksson

Leif Eriksson was one of Eric the Red's sons, born about AD 970. Like his father, Leif was also an explorer. According to Viking sagas he is said to have been the first Viking to set foot in North America. Leif landed in several places and archaeologists have found the remains of a small Viking settlement built at L'Anse aux Meadows (Canada) about 1010 (see page 31). Unfortunately it can't be proved that this was Leif Eriksson's settlement – perhaps one day some new evidence will be unearthed to show that it was.

Fact File

Coins and currency

Coins were an important part of Viking Age economics. Coins made of silver and gold were used to pay 'Danegeld' (see page 27). Arabic silver coins were collected on long-distance travels and taken back to Scandinavia to be melted down or worn as items of jewellery. Thousands and thousands of Arabic coins have been found in Scandinavia.

In England evidence for making coins in the Viking Age has been found at York on the excavations at Coppergate (see page 15). Archaeologists discovered two iron punches called 'dies'. Each die was engraved with the design for a coin. A skilled metal-worker called a 'moneyer' would have been in charge of stamping out coins from strips of sheet silver using the dies, one die for each side of the coin. The dies date from about AD 950 and are the only ones to have survived from the Viking Age. Because moneyers sometimes put their initials or names on coins they made, we can learn even more about actual people of the Viking Age.

An iron punch or 'die' for stamping out silver coins. It was found at York and was used to strike silver pennies during the 950s. The coins were struck on to strips of thin silver and were then cut out with metal clippers.

▲ As king of England, and a Christian, Cnut gave many gifts to cathedrals and churches. This illustration was made about 1031 and it shows Cnut and Emma, his wife, presenting a golden altar cross to Winchester Cathedral. Cnut lived in Winchester when he stayed in England, which is where he was buried in 1035.

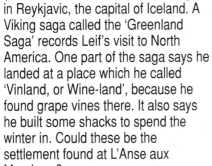

This modern statue of Leif Eriksson ▶ (who was also called Leif the Lucky) is in Reykjavic, the capital of Iceland. A Viking saga called the 'Greenland Saga' records Leif's visit to North America. One part of the saga says he landed at a place which he called 'Vinland, or Wine-land', because he found grape vines there. It also says he built some shacks to spend the winter in. Could these be the settlement found at L'Anse aux Meadows?

Cnut the Great

Cnut (also spelled Canute) was a Viking warrior king who ruled England, Scotland, Denmark and Norway. He was born about AD 995 in Denmark. A saga describes him as, 'exceptionally tall and strong, and the handsomest of men except for his nose which was thin, high-set and rather hooked'. Cnut was a Christian king and had been to Rome on a pilgrimage. During his time as king of England there was peace. After his death in 1035 quarrels broke out between his rivals. In 1066 England was invaded by an army from Normandy (France) made up of soldiers some of whom some were descended from Vikings (see page 27).

Women and children

What was it like for women and children during the Viking Age? Viking women could not become leaders in the true sense – only men were allowed to become kings. But we know from archaeological and historical evidence that women did reach powerful positions in Viking society. The women buried in the great ship at Oseberg must have been people of importance, otherwise why were they given such a lavish burial (see page 23)? And when Cnut married the English queen Emma, the widow of King Ethelred, he did so knowing that she was respected by her English subjects and therefore they would probably respect him too (see page 35).

Life for most ordinary Viking women consisted of household and farming duties. Women tended to animals and made butter and cheese. Inside the long-house they spun wool and wove it into clothes for their family. Some women travelled with their husbands when they were away on raids or trading expeditions – but this was unusual. They may have gone with their menfolk with the intention of settling in new lands.

Viking children were expected to help their parents around the house from an early age. The Vikings did not have schools for their children and if they had any education at all then it was done within the family. There were few toys to play with and those that archaeologists have found are miniature versions of adult objects such as ships, weapons and tools. Viking children were brought up for life in the adult world from a young age.

Viking textiles and raw materials found in York: yarn (top left), silk (top right), wool twill (bottom left and right) and raw wool (bottom centre).

A replica of a Viking loom and loom weights (stones) to hold the threads tight. Looms like this were used by women inside long-houses for weaving clothes.

Viking women were skilled needleworkers, as the detail in this tapestry shows. The three figures represent the gods Odin (one-eyed and holding an axe), Thor (holding a hammer), and Frey (holding a plant). ▶

Fact File

People's names

Names were chosen for children by their fathers. They chose names associated with good luck, or names that had belonged to relatives. Often a child would be given the name of a god – thereby ensuring protection from evil forces. Names based on the god Thor were Thorwald and Thorkel. Some people were given animal names such as Orm (snake), Ulf (wolf) and Björn (bear). The Vikings did not use surnames in the same way that we do, instead they used names that showed family ties such as 'son of' or 'daughter of'. A good example can be seen in the names of Eric Thorwaldsson which means 'Eric, the son of Thorwald' and in his own son's name, Leif Eriksson, which means 'Leif, the son of Eric'. Nick-names were also used. Eric Thorwaldsson's nick-name 'Eric the Red' is better known than his real name. Other equally descriptive (and amusing) Viking nick-names include Ivar the Boneless, Ragnar Hairy Breeches and Harald Bluetooth.

These beads are made of amber, a material formed from fossilized pine resin millions of years ago and washed up on Baltic Sea beaches. The beads were found in York, and may have been a prized possession of a Viking woman. ▶

Replicas of Viking wooden bowls and clay pots. Vessels such as these would have been used for cooking, serving and storing food. ▶

RELIGION AND RITUALS

Gods, goddesses and legends

The early Vikings were pagans - they worshipped many different gods and goddesses. They had three main gods: Odin (the chief god), Thor and Frey. The Vikings believed their gods lived in a place called Asgard. They thought of Asgard as a fortress in the middle of which was a mighty ash tree called Yggdrasil, the 'tree of life'. The tree's roots stretched down to the underworld and its branches reached up to the heavens. According to legend, all the world's rivers flowed from a single spring at the foot of this tree. Another spring was the source of Odin's wisdom.

There was a strong belief in mythical creatures, such as mischievous trolls, dangerous serpents, and a race of frost giants who were the enemies of the gods.

The Vikings didn't have any special buildings in which to practise their religion – the idea of having a special place of worship never seems to have occurred to them. Instead they held their religious meetings in the open air in a field, a clearing in a wood or near to notable landmarks such as a large boulder or a spring of water.

The religion of the Vikings existed at the same time as Christianity was spreading across Europe. Towards the end of the Viking Age many Vikings turned away from their traditional pagan gods and became Christians (see page 43).

Trolls were bad-tempered creatures who liked to trick the gods.

Frigg was the queen of the gods, and was married to Odin. The English word Friday comes from 'Frigg's Day'.

Odin was the chief Viking god. He was the god of knowledge and war and he travelled on an eight-legged horse called Sleipnir. Odin had only one eye. He lost his other eye in a search for knowledge. On his journeys he was escorted by two black ravens, Hugin (Thought) and Munin (Memory). They flew into the world each day and gathered information for Odin which they whispered in his ears.

This object (called Thor's hammer) represents a lightning bolt which the Vikings believed the god Thor could create. This one was worn as a lucky charm.

◀ **Jormungand** was a gigantic serpent who could encircle the world and threaten the gods.

Fact File

Sacrifices to the gods

Viking religion had many rituals some of which seem to have included sacrifices of animals and people. According to a writer who we call Adam of Bremen (Bremen is a city in northern Germany), sacrifices were made by the Vikings at certain times only – to Thor in times of danger from famine or plague, to Odin in time of war and to Frey at the time of a wedding. Adam also recorded that once every nine years humans and animals were sacrificed at a great ceremony in Sweden. Their blood was offered to the gods and their bodies were then hung from nearby trees. Carvings found on stones and even a tapestry buried with the Oseberg ship (see page 23) bear out Adam's grim account, as they show people hanging dead from trees.

Thor was Odin's son. His name meant 'thunder' and he rode through the sky in a chariot pulled by two goats. Thor carried a hammer called Mjöllnir which was the symbol of lightning. As he travelled through the sky he was accompanied by the roar of thunder. The Vikings believed Thor protected them from cold, hunger, giants and other dangers. The English word Thursday comes from his name.

Freyja was the goddess of love and beauty. She liked jewellery and owned a necklace that was called Brisingamen. She travelled through the sky in a chariot drawn by two cats.

Death and burial

Archaeology is about people – not just objects that are dug up. It's certainly not about treasure – well, not in the sense that most people understand. The real 'treasure' of the past is information – finding out what life might have been like hundreds and even thousands of years ago. There's one place where archaeologists make exciting discoveries and where they literally come face to face with people from long ago – cemeteries.

Several Viking cemeteries have been carefully excavated. Because the Vikings practised a pagan religion they were buried with goods intended for use in the afterlife. The practice of burying grave goods with the dead stopped once the Vikings became Christians. Some graves in Viking cemeteries were made in the shape of boats. This shows how important the Vikings felt boats were to them.

Not all Vikings were buried. Some were cremated, as in the case of a Swedish chieftain who died in Russia in about AD 922. His funeral ceremony was witnessed by an Arab traveller called Ibn Fadlan who wrote the details down.

The chieftain had died a few days before the ceremony took place. At first he was buried in a temporary grave with food and possessions. His boat was dragged from the river and firewood

A picture stone which shows a Viking warrior on his journey by boat and horse to Valhalla. In front of the horse is a woman known as a Valkyrie. She was a warrior who decided which soldiers were brave and could therefore enter Valhalla.

This hollowed-out horn, often called a 'horn of plenty', was found buried with a Viking warrior in Sweden. Inside was a collection of silver coins and jewellery, the prized possessions of the dead man.

▲ A Viking cemetery at Lindholm in Denmark. Here, about 200 graves are marked with stones set in the shape of boats. This custom may have been to represent the passage of the dead person's spirit from this world into the next world, on board a boat. (See page 45 for the excavation of a boat burial.)

A Viking warrior, buried with his ▶ weapons, ready to fight again in Valhalla.

Fact File

Valhalla

Valhalla was the home of the god Odin (see page 38). Another name for this place was the 'Hall of the Slain'. Warriors who had died in battle were brought to Valhalla by women called Valkyries, the most famous of whom was Brynhild. The Valkyries were Odin's daughters and their name meant 'Choosers of the Slain' – the 'slain' being the dead Viking warriors. In Valhalla the warriors lived an ideal life: fighting by day and feasting by night. Despite any wounds they may have received they could never be killed. This cycle of fighting and eating carried on in the mythical Valhalla for all eternity.

placed all around it. Then, on the day of the ceremony, the chieftain's body was dug up and dressed in specially-made clothes. His body was placed on the deck of his ship, beneath a small tent. Food was laid around him as were all his weapons. Sacrifices of horses, dogs and cows were made and their bodies thrown into the boat. A slave girl had volunteered to be sacrificed, so she could go with her master into the next world and wait on him. She was strangled and put next to the chieftain. Amid the noise of sticks beating on shields and people singing, the wooden ship was set alight. The funeral fire was kept burning until all that remained was ash.

Discovering the Vikings

In the 1970s this place was a deep, muddy hole in the centre of York. It was the site of the Coppergate Viking excavation – see page 14. Today, a visitor centre stands on the site, where people can see Viking objects found in the excavation and where they can travel along a reconstructed street in the Viking town of Jorvik, deep beneath the modern streets of York.

Our knowledge of the Vikings has grown an amazing amount in the last 100 years. Thanks to some spectacular discoveries and incredible skills of excavation and, just as importantly, conservation techniques (which means looking after things once they've been dug up), we really can see what a Viking long-ship was like, as with the one found at Oseberg (see page 23).

From deep beneath the city streets of modern European and Scandinavian towns has come vital evidence that tells us about the Vikings who lived there 1,000 years ago. Who would have guessed as recently as the early 1970s that several metres under the modern city of York, England, lay the Viking town of Jorvik? From its waterlogged ground thousands of Viking objects came to light in what became known simply as the 'Viking Dig'.

Perhaps one of the biggest discoveries about the Vikings has been made in science laboratories, not on archaeological digs. By studying large pieces of preserved timber, and looking closely at their tree rings, it is sometimes possible to work out the exact year in which the tree was felled. This date will be very close to the year in which a Viking building or timber object was made.

There must be many more Viking surprises to be found and each little scrap of information will help us to understand these Scandinavian adventurers and explorers.

Reconstructing one of the Roskilde Viking boats (see page 24). Traditional wood-working techniques are used and much has been learned about Viking boat-building from work such as this.

▲ Excavation of a small Viking boat on the Orkney island of Sanday in 1991. The boat was on the shoreline and the rough seas were washing it away, so archaeologists had to work quickly. Although the timbers of the boat had rotted away, it was still possible to work out the shape and size of the boat which was nearly 7 metres long. Three Vikings had been buried inside the boat, a man, a woman and a child. Were they Viking settlers who had met with a disaster at sea and had then been buried in their boat? Found with their bodies were a sword, a quiver of arrows, a pair of scissors, a sickle and 22 pieces from the game of 'hnefatafl'. The most spectacular find was a whalebone plaque thought to be an ironing board. It can be seen lying just in front of the man wearing the red hat. (See page 10 for a close-up picture.)

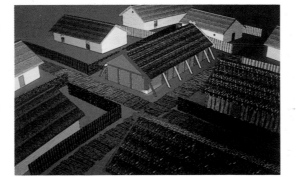

Fact File

Words and place-names

One thing the Vikings took with them wherever they travelled was their language. Today, in parts of England and northern Europe the names of towns, villages and geographical features can be linked to Viking words. Historians and archaeologists use them as evidence that Vikings had once been in those areas. Place-names with Viking links are quite literally 'signposts to the past'! In northern England, in the region once part of the Danelaw (see page 26) there are several places whose names end in '-thwaite'. This word was originally a Scandinavian word that meant a meadow or a clearing in a wood. In the same area the word 'beck' is used to describe a stream, and this too is of Scandinavian origin, as is 'toft' which means a farm. Other words which we now take for granted came into the English language from Scandinavian words, such as 'law', 'egg', 'bread', and believe it or not, 'berserk' which is from an Icelandic word used to describe a rampaging warrior!

◀ A computer generated image of Hedeby, a Viking trading town in Denmark. Computers are used by archaeologists to build up a clear picture of the past.

GLOSSARY

Amber – A fossilized tree sap from pine trees. Used to make jewellery.

Ingolfur Arnarson - The first Viking settler on Iceland.

Asgard – The home of the Viking gods.

Bayeux – A town in northern France where a tapestry was made to record the invasion of England in 1066 by the Normans.

Berserker – A Viking warrior.

Birka – A busy Viking port in Sweden.

Bjarni Herjulfsson – A Viking explorer who was the first European to sight America in the AD 980s. He never landed on the 'new' continent.

Brisingamen – The necklace worn by the goddess Freyja.

Cnut – A Danish Viking who became king of England in 1016.

Coppergate – A street in York (Jorvik), England, where an excavation in the 1970s uncovered buildings and objects from the Viking town. The Jorvik Viking Centre now stands on the spot.

Danegeld – Money and valuables which the Vikings collected from people in exchange for peace. It means 'Danes' gold'.

Danelaw – A large area of England which came under Viking control.

Drakkar – A longship, also called a 'dragon ship'.

Eric the Red – An explorer from Norway who built settlements on Greenland.

Leif Eriksson – A son of Eric the Red who sailed to North America in about 1010.

Fjord – A deep, narrow piece of water that leads to the sea. A Norwegian word.

Freyja – The goddess of love and beauty.

Frigg – The queen of the Viking gods.

Futhark – The Viking alphabet.

Hedeby – A large Viking town in Denmark.

Hnefatafl – A board game played with counters.

Hugin – One of the two ravens that travelled with the god Odin. The name means Thought.

Jelling stone – A rune stone at Jelling, Denmark, recording the conversion of the Danish Vikings to Christianity.

Jorvik – The Viking name for the present-day city of York, in England.

Jormungand - A huge serpent who could encircle the world and threaten the gods.

Kennings – Made-up names for objects, used in sagas.

Knörr – A long-distance merchant ship.

L'Anse aux Meadows – A small Viking settlement in Newfoundland, Canada.

Long-house – A farmhouse which was long and narrow.

Maes Howe – A prehistoric burial mound on the island of Orkney, Scotland. Inside are Viking runes.

Mjöllnir – The hammer carried by the god Thor. It was the symbol of lightning.

Moneyer – A person who made coins.

Munin – One of the two ravens that travelled with the god Odin. The name means Memory.

Norse – The language the Vikings spoke.

Odin – The king of the Viking gods.

Oseberg – A place in Norway where a Viking ship was found buried in 1903.

Roskilde – A place in Denmark where several Viking ships were found in the 1960s.

Runes – The sixteen letters of the Viking alphabet.

Saga – A long story or poem.

Skalds – Storytellers who recited sagas.

Sleipnir – The eight-legged horse ridden by Odin.

Thing – An open-air meeting at which disputes were settled, laws made and taxes collected.

Thor – A warrior god whom the Vikings believed protected them from evil forces.

Eric Thorwaldsson – see Eric the Red.

Trolls – Bad-tempered creatures who played tricks on the gods.

Up-Hella-Aa – A modern fire festival held at Lerwick, Shetland, where a replica Viking boat is burnt each January.

Valhalla – The place where the god Odin lived and where warriors went after they died.

Valkyrie – Female warriors who chose the bravest fighters to enter Valhalla.

Wattle and daub – Inter-woven twigs and poles covered with a thick coat of clay, straw and manure. A popular method of house building in Viking and later times.

Yggdrasil – The giant ash tree which the Vikings believed held up the world.

INDEX

FURTHER READING

If you want to find out more about the Vikings, these books will help:

The Vikings At A Glance, Mike Corbishley (Macdonald Young Books, 1998)
The Vikings, Louise James (Heinemann, 1997)
Vikings, Fiona Macdonald (Oxford University Press, 1992)
Myths and Civilization of the Vikings, Hazel Mary Martell (Watts, 1998)
Everyday Life in Viking Times, Hazel Mary Martell (Watts, 1993)
How Would You Survive as a Viking?, Jacqueline Morley (Watts, 1993)